But God...

A 30-Day Journey of HOPE!

But God...

A 30-Day Journey of HOPE!

The Story of Well-Grounded Coffee Community

Tell a Different Story.
Tell a Better Story.
Tell a Victory Story.

Natalie Huscheck
& The Well Grounded Sisterhood

PERFORMANCE
PUBLISHING

Thank You to our Top Sponsors (and great friends)

GOLD SPONSORS
Anna Seo & Harry Kim

SILVER SPONSORS
Anthony Wright
Owner: Safe Hands Insurance

Annetta Wright
Founder/Owner: Transformative
Marketing Solutions, LLC

BRONZE SPONSORS
Restored Hope
501c3 Partner

Jesse Simmons
Owner: Jesse's AC & Appliance

Michael DeGroat
Financial Advisor: Ameriprise Financial

A WORD
FROM
SUSAN STEPHENS
DIRECTOR, EXODUS MINISTRIES

Exodus Ministries is an intensive, comprehensive, residential, one-year program for single mothers and their children. All of our mothers have been previously incarcerated. This program is designed to provide the foundational building blocks the women missed along the way. It is an intense program that includes mandatory life-skills classes, Christian Counseling, assigned chores on property, church attendance, and getting a job. Our goal is to give these children their mothers back, help the women learn how to live differently and become responsible, contributing members of society, and show them that they matter and they are worthy, Jesus loves them, and their past does not define their future.

When I met Natalie at a local networking group, we connected right away. Our love for Jesus and our hearts for the marginalized in society brought us together. Our desire to help other women discover and embrace their value and worth inspired us to link arms and work together to bring opportunities to women.

It was Natalie's dream that caused her to set up multiple meetings to ask about our ministry, how it worked, and what it might look like if they could create a coffee shop to employ our women. It was her persistence, creativity, tenacity, and passion that inspired me and drove me to imagine ways we could work together that would be mutually beneficial.

Well Grounded Community Coffee embodies the values we embrace. Giving second chances and seeing people as redeemable, valuable, and worthy is who we are and what we are each called to do. God has modeled this for all of us. He has redeemed us, continues to give us second, third, and fourth chances, and reminds us that we are all valuable and worthy of His love.

The women who work at Well Grounded Community Coffee are taught valuable life skills, partnered with Mentors, challenged to be their best selves, and valued for who God created them to be. It has sparked joy, given them a sense of belonging and value, and inspired them to chase their dreams.

Our partnership with WGCC has changed lives, inspired growth, and set these women on a path of independence, self-sufficiency and the ability to provide for their families. They have been blessed immensely and will never be the same. It has been my joy and privilege to work with Natalie and Michael as they provide mentorship in personal growth as well as job skills for these women. I am humbled and honored to be able to link arms and work together in such a significant, life-changing endeavor.

In His Grip and for His Glory,
Susan Stephens
Executive Director
Exodus Ministries

A WORD FROM FATHER GREG BOYLE

FOUNDER, HOMEBOY INDUSTRIES
AUTHOR OF TATTOOS
ON THE HEART

God's dream come true is the formation of a community of cherished belonging. If it's true that a traumatized person may well cause trauma, then it has to be equally true that a cherished person will be able to find their way to the joy there is in cherishing themselves and others. The women of the Well Grounded Coffee Community are saved by their stories. Equally, we are not saved from ourselves in hearing them, but saved to ourselves. We are all returned to our true selves in loving by receiving these stories to enhance our own prayer. We discover in them that loving is our home. Knowing that means we will never be homesick again. Kinship, such that God might recognize it, is God's dream come true.

A WORD
FROM
RICHARD MILES
FOUNDER, MILES OF FREEDOM

"Count it all joy, my brothers [and sisters] when you meet trials of various kinds. For you know that the testing of your faith produces patience." (James 1:2 ESV)

Life will present challenges to each of us, and how we work through "life challenges" will ultimately define our character and perception of life. At our core, we are human beings created to experience "life" while embracing its highs and lows. We're all gifted with a measure of "hope" and "optimism" that is fueled when our faith is activated and manifested. We will encounter individuals along this journey who will pour into us the resources needed to sustain the positive outlook to be courageous and great. It's an honor to know and work with the family of "Well Grounded," Well Grounded has seized the opportunity to not only change the "look" and "taste" of life but also the quality of living. Such as the coffee bean seed that not only enhances the taste of water but also provides energy to those who partake.

It is an extreme honor and privilege to provide words of encouragement and credibility to the work of "Well Grounded." As partners in the space of serving others, Miles of Freedom is excited to know others working in the vineyard of redemption and vindication. We look forward to all of the exciting things on the horizon for "Well Grounded" and are proud partners in this space.

Thank you for an opportunity to be a part of this beautiful devotion. We pray that our work, testimony, and truths go with each of you today. Fret Not - Count It All Joy.

Respectfully,
Richard R. Miles Jr
Miles of Freedom
Founder, President/CEO

INTRODUCTION
EXCERPT FROM OSWALD CHAMBERS, MY UTMOST FOR HIS HIGHEST, JULY 6TH

> God gives us a vision, and then He takes us down to the valley to batter us into the shape of that vision. It is in the valley that so many of us give up and faint. Every God-given vision will become real if we will only have patience. Just think of the enormous amount of free time God has! He is never in a hurry. Yet we are always in such a frantic hurry. While still in the light of the glory of the vision, we go right out to do things, but the vision is not yet real in us. God has to take us into the valley and put us through fires and floods to batter us into shape, until we get to the point where He can trust us with the reality of the vision.

I love this message. I'm not 100% sold on the theological accuracy of it. I might have said that the world takes us down into the valley. God allows it. He uses the difficulties of this world to help mold us. Either way, His molding was exactly what I experienced in the process of dreaming, creating, and building our non-profit. The vision began at least a decade before we ever opened the doors of Well Grounded Coffee Community, and what a ride!

Background

I was born in Cincinnati, Ohio, the third of four children. I was raised in the Catholic Church, and I never remember a time when I did not believe in God. He was always real to me, albeit distant and a bit fearsome. I never doubted His existence. What I didn't know about was how to have a meaningful relationship with His Son, Jesus. It would be years before I realized that in Christ,

I am seen. I am safe. I am significant.

These are our stories. With our hope placed in God, we are re-writing our stories. Although they began with trauma, abuse, drugs, prison, lies, and more, that doesn't define who we are and what our futures look like. Each of us has chosen to:

Tell a Different Story, a Better Story, a Victory Story!
We hope you will be inspired to do the same.
501(c)(3): The Dignity Project – established in 2019
DBA: Well Grounded Coffee Community
– opened November 2020

Mission

Transforming lives through a process of work, education, community, and faith, The Dignity Project DBA: Well Grounded Coffee Community will create opportunities for individuals who are barely surviving life to reach a higher level of purpose and social contribution.

4 Pillars
Work. Education. Community. Faith.

"Speak up for those who cannot speak for themselves; ensure justice for those being crushed. Yes, speak up for the poor and helpless, and see that they get justice." **(Proverbs 31:8-9 NLT)**

Hiring Partners:
Exodus Ministries
In My Shoes
Nexus/Oxford House/Magdalen House
Restored Hope

CONTENTS

DAY 1

Natalie's Story:
Adventure & Anxiety

"Do not be anxious about anything, but in every
situation, by prayer and petition, with thanksgiving,
present your requests to God. And the peace of God,
which transcends all understanding, will guard your
hearts and your minds in Christ Jesus."
(Philippians 4:6-7 NIV)

Growing up, my life was unexceptional in most ways. My family was fairly normal and somewhat dysfunctional, as many families are! And then, during the summer before my third grade year, we moved from the city to rural Indiana. My family, along with my dad's business partner, purchased over 100 acres of woods and farmland, and we built a small A-framed house. This radical change for me was both terrifying and pure adventure, and we spent our free time exploring the land, woods, creeks, ponds, barn, etc. We were on our own a lot, and I remember an ever-present feeling of anxiety and "not safe," and yet there seemed to always be new kittens to search for and a runaway goat to chase down. It was a strange mix of feeling fearful and excited all at once. Generalized anxiety was my constant companion.

As I grew into adulthood, my life continued with this strange mix of faith, adventure, and high anxiety. After college, I spent a year in Venezuela working with malnourished children and their families. When I came back to the States, I met and married a youth pastor, and we started a family as well as a church. We had three beautiful daughters, and we adopted a sibling group of four boys from the foster care system. Our lives were full. I felt mostly exhilarated and a little bit overwhelmed. What I didn't realize was that my husband was dying under the weight of our lives. My family began to crumble and fall apart. Darkness entered. Paired with that feeling of "unsafe."

My husband began staying away from home more and more. When he was home, he was angry, stressed, and aggressive. At his worst, he would rage and throw things. Our home began to feel less and less safe... wait, had it ever felt safe? One day, when two of our boys got into a physical fight, he lost his temper and began to rage. At that moment, my eyes were opened to the level of "un-health" in my marriage and family. It was like a light switch clicked on. I could no longer bury the feeling by pretending that everything was okay. I took the girls to a safe place and sought counseling. Three of the boys had already moved out. James, the youngest, stayed. I truly believed we could reconcile, but in the end, he filed for divorce.

The raging and eventual divorce sent me into a very dark season of my life. I thought I would feel relief to be away from his anger, but the shame of failure and abandoning the boys overshadowed any possible feelings of relief. Suddenly, I was a divorced, single mom. Yet it was during this dark season that God began to fill my mind with a vision to uplift and encourage other women in darkness to reach out to others who felt unseen, unsafe, and insignificant.

Question: Have you experienced anxiety, the feeling of "unsafe," or darkness in your life?

What are some words you would use to describe what your worst moments have felt like?

The lie: I am unlovable.

The truth: "And so we know and rely on the love God has for us. God is love. Whoever lives in love lives in God, and God in them." (1 John 4:16 NIV)

Prayer: Father, help me to trade the lies from the enemy and the world for Your truth. You chose me. You love me. You sent Your Son for me that I may have life, and life abundant. The truth about me is what YOU say about me. And You say I am loved. Seal this in my heart. Amen.

DAY 2

Natalie's Story:
Darkness

"Not only so, but we also glory in our sufferings,
because we know that suffering produces perseverance;
perseverance, character; and character, HOPE."
(Romans 5:3-4 NIV)

Being a single mom, I worked two or three jobs to make ends meet while struggling to be home before and after school for my three little girls. We lived in constant financial struggle. At times, we had the electricity or water turned off. At other times, we had to move in with my parents. My car was repossessed. Yet we pressed on. I prayed, and I journaled.

One of the jobs I worked at was in sales and marketing. One day, I was on a training call, pacing my room, growing more and more agitated. The trainer was announcing different sales achievements. At the end of each success, we were supposed to cheer loudly. It felt inauthentic, so I hung up the phone. I had never done something like that before. I thought to myself, "I'm not happy for those people. I'm jealous. Why can't I succeed?" It was a terrible feeling to feel stuck and ashamed to admit my shallowness, even to myself. On a reflex, I called a friend, who was a life coach, to process the incident. After explaining what happened, she asked me some hard questions.

Friend: "Natalie, do you want me to help you understand why you aren't happy for those people?"

Me: "Yes."

Friend: "You are stuck in a victim mindset. You cannot achieve victory with a victim mindset. What do you think is the payoff for 'playing the victim?'"

Me: "Payoff? What? I don't know."

Friend: "There must be a payoff if you are choosing the mindset of victim over victory. Are you looking for sympathy? Do you have a strong need to be right? What do you think the payoff is?"

Me: "I've never thought about it."

Friend: "I encourage you to think about it and to make the DECISION to give up your sad stories, stop blaming others, and fight for victory. You can't have it both ways. This includes celebrating other people's victories."

Me: "Ouch."

My friend's hard but honest words were like a second light switch in my mind. I made a clear decision at that moment to give up my sad stories, stop blaming, and journey with others toward a life of victory. Once again, God impressed upon me the idea of lifting others out of darkness (and their own victim mentality). But what would that even look like?

I continued praying and journaling, asking God how I could find my way out of darkness, much less lead others to light.

Mostly, I still felt unseen, unsafe, and insignificant.

Questions: Have you ever received hard words from a friend?

Do you think they meant harm or good?

Regardless of how they were meant, how can you use the words to grow and reach toward victory?

The lie: I am helpless. I will fail.

The truth: "I can do all things through Him who strengthens me." (Philippians 4:13 ESV).

Prayer: Dear Lord, on my own, I have failed, but I am no longer on my own. My life is in You, and You have endless strength. You have all the power. Help me remember to call on You for guidance and strength every day from moment to moment. Amen.

DAY 3

Natalie's Story: Finding the Light

But God,
being rich in mercy, because of His great love with which He loved us, even when we were dead in our transgressions, made us alive together with Christ (by grace you have been saved), and raised us up with Him, and seated us with Him in the heavenly *places* in Christ Jesus, so that in the ages to come He might show the surpassing riches of His grace in kindness toward us in Christ Jesus. For by grace you have been saved through faith; and that not of yourselves, *it is* the gift of God;
(Ephesians 2:4-8 NASB1995)

As I continued to press into God, my life began to transform. I married an amazing man named Michael. We had a baby boy together. My three daughters grew into beautiful, caring young women. And I began trying to rebuild relationships with my adopted boys. On my journey to live and teach victory, we were making plans to open a non-profit coffee house to give second chances to marginalized women in Dallas. We were stuck financially because we imagined the non-profit with housing where the baristas would live together in a supportive community. Finding a property that included residential and commercial space was difficult and expensive. Then I met the director of Exodus Ministries, and I realized that by partnering with them, we could move forward without the housing part.

Exodus Ministries is a transitional home for formerly incarcerated moms. The moms are reunited with their children, given an apartment, and sent out to get jobs. That's where we would come in. We would offer the women jobs with a career path, educational opportunities, a community of people, resources, and spiritual support for a strong foundation — basically, a pathway to a better life for them and their kids, a path of victory.

We formed a 501(c)(3) non-profit named The Dignity Project, and our first DBA (doing business as) was a coffee house called Well Grounded Coffee Community. We found an amazing location in East Dallas and secured the lease. By the Fall of 2020, we were in the middle of the build-out for Well Grounded. We had interviewed and hired two beautiful women from Exodus Ministries.

As build-outs often do, this one was dragging on far beyond all promised deadlines, and I was becoming very anxious.

Since we had already hired the two women and they had left their previous jobs (at Jimmy Johns and Sonic), we decided to have them come in and help with some light decorating, painting, and moving of furniture. One of the most fun parts of decorating was watching the space transform into a place of victory. Each part of the design had a story. For example, Highland Park Cafeteria, a Dallas icon, had gone out of business due to the COVID-19 pandemic, and we were able to buy the wood from their walls, as well as tables, chairs, and lights, which brought some warmth and history to Well Grounded. In the process, we developed a wonderful friendship with the former owner of Highland Park Cafeteria, Jeff Snoyer.

Day by day, as we worked together, the place became a safe haven for the baristas and the community to grow together.

As the build-out continued to lag, we had to move the coffee training to my home. Okay, let's face it — inviting a couple of felons that I barely knew into my home may not have been considered the smartest decision, but it built trust. Was it risky? Yes, but this was merely the first of many risks we took in the name of giving second chances.

Most importantly, I was learning that in Christ,
I was seen, I was safe, and I was significant.

**Lifting others out of darkness —
This is my Victory Story!**

Tell a New Story. Tell a Better Story. Tell a Victory Story!

DAY 4

Natasha's Story:
Demons & Numbing

"Jesus traveled about from one town and
village to another, proclaiming the good news
of the kingdom of God. The Twelve were with him,
and also some women who had been cured of evil spirits
and diseases: Mary (called Magdalene) from whom
seven demons had come out;"
(Luke 8:1-2 NIV)

Natasha was one of the first two baristas we hired in November of 2020. A quiet, meek redhead with a humble spirit, she had certainly faced many demons in her lifetime. Tasha lacked confidence in herself in most areas but was eager to learn. She was easy to teach and easier to love. She was fascinated with the coffee world even though she had spent her time in prison drinking only instant coffee. (Truth be told, she might even sneak in a cup of instant once in a while today!)

Tasha was born in Galveston, TX, and grew up in Vidor, TX. Although her parents did marry, she has no childhood memory of them together. She describes her father as being like a ghost. He would get close enough for her to see him, and then he was gone. Her mom had many boyfriends over the years, but Tasha does remember one very present stepdad. He was an alcoholic and physically abusive to her mom and siblings. Her older sister would hide Tasha and her younger brother in a closet to protect them From the abuse. Tasha's mom was on and off drugs throughout her childhood, and by the age of twelve, Tasha began using drugs herself. By age sixteen, she was using IV drugs. She became pregnant and had her first child at the age of fifteen. Tasha's mom signed the papers for her to marry the baby's father, who was a much older man of forty-five. Both her mom and husband pressured her to abort the baby, but Tasha had hopes that the father would grow to love her and the baby and they could be a family. This did not happen, and the marriage ended. Tasha continued on a broken path of drugs and bad relationships.

Tasha's mom also continued down this broken path and died when Tasha was only twenty-one years old. Her dad, who continued to be ghostlike, was in and out of jail. Her paternal grandma, who played a significant role in her life, died in 2017, a major loss for her. With so much trauma and pain in her life, Tasha learned how to numb her emotions as a simple matter of survival. The human soul can only bear so much hardship.

Questions: Do you know what it's like to "numb" yourself?

Are you willing to allow yourself to feel the discomfort of emotional pain and release it to God?

What do you use to numb yourself? Drugs or alcohol? Food? Isolation? Other?

The lie: I am helpless. Numbing is the only way I can survive this life.

The truth: "Blessed be the God and Father of our Lord Jesus Christ, the Father of mercies and God of all comfort, who comforts us in all our affliction, so that we may be able to comfort those who are in any affliction, with the comfort with which we ourselves are comforted by God. For as we share abundantly in Christ's sufferings, so through Christ we share abundantly in comfort too." (2 Corinthians 1:3-5 NASB1995)

Prayer: Daddy, God, You are good. You are safe. You will comfort me and allow me to comfort others! Show me how to receive Your love and comfort. Show me how to feel the pain and lift it up to You for healing, a little at a time. You are safe. You are loved. Let me rest in You. Amen.

DAY 5

Natasha's Story: In Prison & Pregnant

"This is what the LORD says to you:
'Do not be afraid or discouraged because of this vast
army. For the battle is not yours, but God's.'"
(2 Chronicles 20:15b NIV)

In 2018, Tasha was sent to prison for "evading arrest." She had spent time in jail before, but this sentence was likely to be significantly longer. In her downward spiral, she had lost custody of several children. Her oldest son was being raised by her grandma and aunt. Her son, Matthew, was being raised by her younger brother.

She found out at "book-in" at the county jail that she was pregnant again. As shocked as she was, Tasha says it was this pregnancy that God used to turn her life around. She knew she had to find a different path. She gave birth to Samuel with four months left to serve. She felt certain she would lose custody of him too, but miraculously, the baby's paternal grandma took him in while she finished her time.

She left prison and was accepted into Exodus Ministries. Two days after settling at Exodus, her son, Samuel, was brought to her. With her own apartment and more stability and support than she had ever experienced, she began to see a light in the darkness. She looked around the apartment and thought, "This is the way normal people live." But she had never felt normal. She had never felt worthy of a "normal" life.

Questions: Have you lost a child from death, abortion, or custody?

Are you willing to trust God with the pain and accept His total forgiveness?

On a scale of 1-10, how much do you believe that God can and will forgive you? (1 is not at all, 10 is completely)

The lie: I am worthless.

The truth: "Therefore if anyone is in Christ, *he is* a new crea-
ture; the old things passed away; behold, new things have
come." (2 Corinthians 5:17 NASB1995)

Prayer: Creator of the universe, thank You for making me
NEW! I am not simply an improved version of my old self;
I am a new creation. Make that truth sink into me. Help me
believe that and live that. I am worthy of Your love because I
am a new creation. Amen.

DAY 6
Natasha's Story:
Learning to FEEL

But God,
being rich in mercy, because of His great love with
which He loved us, even when we were dead in our
transgressions, made us alive together with Christ (by
grace you have been saved), and raised us up with Him,
and seated us with Him in the heavenly *places* in Christ
Jesus, so that in the ages to come He might show the
surpassing riches of His grace in kindness toward us in
Christ Jesus. For by grace you have been saved through
faith; and that not of yourselves, *it is* the gift of God;
(Ephesians 2:4-8 NASB1995)

Tasha began to learn how to live differently, how to parent, how to work. She was hired at Jimmy John's but was only paid minimum wage and given very short shifts. The struggle was intense, using public transportation to take her son to daycare and then another bus to work, working three or four hour shifts. and then doing the whole thing again in reverse. She was learning a new kind of "grit."

Then, in November of 2020, we interviewed and hired her as our very first Barista-in-Training. Tasha was ready to create a new future and really began to grow in confidence after being welcomed into the Well Grounded Coffee Community.

- In May 2021, Tasha earned her first promotion to Tier II Barista with a raise. She trained and took on the role of official store "closer."

- In September of 2021, she earned her second raise and promotion to Tier III Barista. She was also invited to become a board member!

- In January of 2022, Tasha earned her next promotion to Tier IV Barista with a pathway to Store Manager.

Natasha once shared with me that when she was using, she used to think, "Why would anyone choose to go through life and NOT be high?" Numbing was simply her way of life then. Now she was learning a new way.

Part of the process at Well Grounded is learning to feel without numbing. Good and bad feelings are all new and can be scary and uncomfortable. One of the first times I heard Natasha laugh was when a customer ordered a decaf latte.

Pulling a decaf espresso shot is one of the more challenging parts of serving coffee at Well Grounded. It takes extra care and often takes several tries to get it right. She looked at me and said, "Have you ever seen the movie *Coyote Ugly*? You know when someone comes in and orders water, and one of the bartenders shouts out 'water!' and sprays them down with the water hose? Well, that's what I feel like doing when someone orders a decaf!" We both had a good laugh and continued to tell the joke whenever a beloved customer would order the dreaded drink!

Along the way, Tasha moved into her own apartment and began taking college classes. She also started rebuilding her relationships with other family members.

The greatest victory, however, was that she was indeed learning to feel again. Laughter and tears came as we joked daily, mourned the death of her father, and celebrated gaining visits with her middle son, Matthew.

After eighteen months with us, Natasha was hired onto the office staff of another non-profit, where she has the opportunity each day to love on and serve marginalized women in Dallas. We are so VERY proud of Tasha. Her story continues to be lived out in victory, and you can still find her at the cash register or espresso machine on occasional Saturdays at Well Grounded. She continues to sit on our board of directors and is an integral part of making decisions that will help other women heal and learn to live in victory. Most recently, Natasha gained back custody of her ten-year-old son!

"When Jesus rose early on the first day of the week, he appeared first to Mary Magdalene, out of whom he had driven seven demons." (Mark 16:9 NIV)

I love how Jesus spent his time with fishermen, prostitutes, and tax collectors. Basically, he hung out with those whom society had rejected, those who needed a second chance, someone to believe in them. Jesus had certainly given Mary Magdalene a second chance, hope, and a different future. And in the end, when he was resurrected, the FIRST person Jesus appeared to was Mary Magdalene!

Natasha's Advice:

When asked what she would say to others in similar situations, Natasha's response is, "Trust the process. It may seem you aren't getting anywhere, but if you are in a program, class, or transitional home, stick with it and TRUST. THE. PROCESS."

In Christ, Natasha is seen, she is safe, and she is significant!

**Helping others "un-numb" and learn to feel—
This is Natasha's Victory Story!**

Tell a New Story. Tell a Better Story. Tell a Victory Story!

DAY 7

Angela's Story:
Unseen & Unsafe

One of the Pharisees asked Jesus to eat with him, so
Jesus went into the Pharisee's house and sat at the table.
A sinful woman in the town learned that Jesus was eating
at the Pharisee's house. So she brought an alabaster jar
of perfume and stood behind Jesus at his feet, crying.
She began to wash his feet with her tears, and she
dried them with her hair, kissing them many times and
rubbing them with the perfume. When the Pharisee who
asked Jesus to come to his house saw this, he thought to
himself, "If Jesus were a prophet, he would know that
the woman touching him is a sinner!"
(Luke 7: 36-39 NLT)

Angela was born in Carlsbad, New Mexico. At the time of her birth, her parents were married, and she had one older brother. Her parents had another son and then divorced when she was only three. Her dad fought for custody of the three children and won. Although her father loved her and was the source of stability for Angela, he had three more wives after their mom, and none of them were kind to Angela or her brothers. The longest relationship Angela remembers her father having was from the time she was six through the time she was seventeen. This stepmom both physically and emotionally abused her.

Feeling abandoned by her birth mother and rejected and abused by her stepmothers, Angela experienced extreme loneliness and unhappiness throughout her childhood. She spent many years searching for a love that would fill the gap. The message that she was "fat" and that nobody liked "fat girls" felt like the silent theme of her life. Angela remembers crying herself to sleep many nights. In her senior year of high school, she started "smoking weed." She said she just didn't care anymore.

Angela did graduate from high school and moved to California with a friend to continue her search for happiness. However, she became pregnant after a short-term relationship with a marine. When the marine found out she was pregnant, he disclosed that he was married and quickly disappeared from her life. Angela moved back home to her dad. She was a single mom for many years, but when her daughter was in kindergarten, she met a guy and married, still searching to fill the gap left by her mother.

Questions: Have you felt the deep loneliness of abandonment or rejection?

Where do you feel that pain in your body? Stomach? Head? Shoulders? Heart? Other?

What helps you feel less lonely?

The lie: I am unlovable. People will always reject and abandon me.

The truth: "For you are a people holy to the LORD your God. The LORD your God has chosen you out of all the peoples on the face of the earth to be his people, his treasured possession." (Deuteronomy 7:6 NIV)

Prayer: Father, You have chosen me. I am Yours. You will never abandon or reject me. In You, I am holy and perfect. Show me how to receive Your great love and to love myself as You have made me. Amen.

DAY 8

Angela's Story: Abuse, Hopelessness, & Prison

"…weeping may remain for a night,
but rejoicing comes in the morning."
(Psalm 30:5b NASB1995)

Angela managed to earn a massage therapy certification and begin a small business. Meanwhile, her husband started using and selling drugs, and the domestic violence started. Angela also began using more and more drugs to cope with her hopeless situation.

In the midst of this chaos, she had a baby boy named Lukas and became pregnant again when Lukas was only six months old. This second baby boy was born at just seven months as a result of her husband's physical abuse. Although the baby was born alive, his lungs were not strong enough to keep him alive, and she lost him. A few years after that, another baby boy, Jacob, was born.

Sometime between the birth of Lukas and the baby she lost, Angela began looking for a way out of the abusive relationship. Just after the birth of Jacob, she managed to take the boys to Dallas but was arrested for possession of meth and heroin not long after the move. She was sentenced to five years and served 1 ½ years in prison. She nearly lost custody of the two boys, but her daughter, now a young adult, took them in while she finished her sentence. For Angela, prison was terrifying. She felt that she had totally lost control over her life and the lives of her children. This loss of control ultimately turned her toward God. She learned that "God had her back" and that He was there when she had no one else. He took care of her children while she was in prison and gave her peace and comfort when she thought she was going to break down.

Angela was released from prison and within three months applied and was accepted into Exodus Ministries.

Questions: Have you ever chosen a "bad" relationship over being alone?

Which do you believe is worse: staying in a "bad" relationship or being alone?

Are you ready to seek God over bad relationships?

The lie: I am helpless. I cannot get my life under control!

The truth: "Give me your heart, my son,

And let your eyes delight in my ways." (Proverbs 23:26 NASB1995)

Prayer: Dearest Father, You and only You are in control. I surrender my life and my heart completely to You. I have messed up my life, and only You can be trusted with it. Teach me Your ways. I will follow You. Amen.

DAY 9

Angela's Story:
Finding Light & Hope

But God,
being rich in mercy, because of His great love with
which He loved us, even when we were dead in our
transgressions, made us alive together with Christ
(by grace you have been saved), and raised us up
with Him, and seated us with Him in the
heavenly *places* in Christ Jesus, so that in the ages
to come He might show the surpassing riches of His
grace in kindness toward us in Christ Jesus.
For by grace you have been saved through faith;
and that not of yourselves, *it is* the gift of God;
(Ephesians 2:4-8 NASB1995)

Well Grounded hired Angela in January 2021, just a month after the store opened. From the start, she exhibited confidence and an eagerness to please. She came from an abusive (domestic violence) past and had found safe shelter for herself and her two boys at Exodus Ministries. Angela was the grateful type and, just like the woman who washed Jesus' feet, she showed her gratitude openly and passionately. She was excited about everything that Well Grounded had to offer, from dental services to college classes. Angela often spoke for Well Grounded to local groups. She is very intelligent and well-spoken.

While Angela was eager to fit in, she was sometimes abrasive and blunt with her comments and reactions. We still laugh about her initial opinion of our prices: "Well, that's the smallest $6 sandwich I've ever seen!" It was as if Angela was waiting to see if she was safe at Well Grounded, if she could fit in and be accepted, or if she would be rejected, as she had been so many times before.

As Angela came closer to graduating from Exodus Ministries, she was looking for an apartment for her boys and her dad. Her dad was getting older, and Angela felt a great desire to take care of him. Suddenly, her dad became very ill with cancer and died within a month of his diagnosis. Angela grieved the loss of the one family member who had loved and encouraged her. She quickly shifted her focus and found a transitional home for single moms who were willing to attend college full time. Unsurprisingly, Angela became an excellent student, taking business management and accounting classes and achieving a 3.8 GPA in her first year. In the end, Angela fit in so well at Well Grounded that when she moved on to another job, we grieved deeply and begged her to work occasional weekends so we could stay connected.

Angela's new job was in an accounting office, where she began learning how to master every aspect of the business. She and the boys began family counseling, and she set a five-to-ten-year goal of taking over her boss' business when he retires.

Angela does return to work an occasional Saturday at Well Grounded, and she and her boys join us for Team retreats and events!

> Jesus said to the Pharisee, "Simon, I have something to say to you." Simon said, "Teacher, tell me." Jesus said, "Two people owed money to the same banker. One owed five hundred coins and the other owed fifty. They had no money to pay what they owed, but the banker told both of them they did not have to pay him. Which person will love the banker more?" Simon, the Pharisee, answered, "I think it would be the one who owed him the most money." Jesus said to Simon, "You are right." Then Jesus turned toward the woman and said to Simon, "Do you see this woman? When I came into your house, you gave me no water for my feet, but she washed my feet with her tears and dried them with her hair. You gave me no kiss of greeting, but she has been kissing my feet since I came in. You did not put oil on my head, but she poured perfume on my feet. I tell you that her many sins are forgiven, so she showed great love. But the person

> who is forgiven only a little will love only a little." Then Jesus said to her, "Your sins are forgiven." The people sitting at the table began to say among themselves, "Who is this who even forgives sins?" Jesus said to the woman, "Because you believed, you are saved from your sins. Go in peace." (Luke 7:40-50 NLT)

Angela's life is now filled with a peace that she did not have before. She walks in gratitude and encourages others at every opportunity. She is pure joy and has filled the "gap" her mother left with a God relationship.

Angela's Advice:

Be still, let God guide you, and don't make emotional decisions. Listen for His voice and trust it.

In Christ, Angela feels seen, safe, and significant!

Offering hope and encouragement to others — This is Angela's Victory Story!

Tell a New Story. Tell a Better Story. Tell a Victory Story!

DAY 10

Hannah's Story:
Mostly Curious

Jesus, tired as he was from the journey, sat
down by the well. It was about noon.
When a Samaritan woman came to draw water, Jesus
said to her, "Will you give me a drink?" The Samaritan
woman said to him, "You are a Jew and I am a Samaritan
woman. How can you ask me for a drink?" Jesus
answered her, "If you knew the gift of God and who it is
that asks you for a drink, you would have asked him and
he would have given you living water." "Sir," the woman
said, "you have nothing to draw with and the well is
deep. Where can you get this living water?"
(John 4:6-11 NIV)

Hannah was born in Abilene, TX, the younger of two girls. Although the family struggled financially, her dad was a hard worker, and her parents loved her and each other. Hannah remembers her mom drinking when she was very little but that she stopped when Hannah was nine or ten years old due to severe stomach issues.

Overall, Hannah had a stable childhood and did earn a GED at the urging of her mom.

In middle school, out of curiosity, Hannah started experimenting with OxyContin, and she continued popping pills throughout her teen years. She dated an older guy, nineteen years old, from the time she was thirteen until she was sixteen. Hannah grew up in a world where pot smoking was prevalent, so numbing herself seemed normal. She believed that "all adults drank or did some kind of drug in order to numb themselves."

Questions: What are your main addictions? Drugs? Alcohol? Food? Pornography? Other?

Have you ever sought help to overcome these addictions?

The lie: I am helpless. Numbing is necessary for me to get through life.

The truth: "Jesus answered, 'I am the way and the truth and the life. No one comes to the Father except through me.'" (John 14:6 NIV)

Prayer: God, Your Son, Jesus, is life. He is the way. Feeling all the pain is hard. Let me walk in Your truth, one moment at a time, as You heal all the wounds of all the trauma. Let me be courageous enough to feel, and let me cling desperately to You. Amen.

DAY 11

Hannah's Story:
Facing Consequences

"No temptation has overtaken you except
what is common to mankind. And God is faithful;
he will not let you be tempted beyond what you can bear.
But when you are tempted, he will also provide a way
out so that you can endure it."
(1 Corinthians 10:13 NIV)

Living a party/numbing lifestyle led to Hannah becoming pregnant at age seventeen by a guy she barely had a relationship with. Her son, Nathan, was born when she was eighteen. She and Nathan lived with her parents for two years and then moved in with her new boyfriend.

They had lived with her boyfriend for four years when she became pregnant with her second son, Evan. Although Hannah did care deeply for Evan's father, the drugs trumped everything in the end, and she entered a very dark season. Drugs had gone from a curiosity to a crippling force that she could no longer control.

Hannah started using crystal meth at the age of twenty. When Evan was three years old, her drug use elevated to "shooting up" with meth. She had also started selling drugs, and this led to losing custody of Evan to his dad. Her drug use escalated, and Hannah ended up in prison when Evan was just four years old.

Hannah spent a total of 2 1/2 years incarcerated, during which time she felt deeply lonely. After the first year, Hannah says she began having thoughts of changing her life but had no idea if it was possible or how to go about it. After year two and spending the second year in a row missing her sons' birthdays, Hannah began looking for a pathway to change. She found some information about Exodus Ministries and began to see some hope for her future. Hannah was released from prison early in 2021 and moved into her own apartment at Exodus with her son, Nathan, in February of 2021. She was hired at Well Grounded shortly after.

Questions: Have you experienced "darkness" in your life?

Was it mostly the result of your poor choices or someone else's?

The lie: I am worthless. There is no way out for me. This is simply how my life will be forever.

The truth: "We have this hope as an anchor for the soul, firm and secure. It enters the inner sanctuary behind the curtain," (Hebrews 6:19 NIV)

Prayer: Daddy, God, You are my hope. You are an anchor for my soul. In You, there is light, strength, and hope. May Your name be always on my lips and in my heart. Amen.

DAY 12
Hannah's Story: Finding True Joy

But God,
being rich in mercy, because of His great love with
which He loved us, even when we were dead in our
transgressions, made us alive together with Christ
(by grace you have been saved), and raised us up with
Him, and seated us with Him in the heavenly *places*
in Christ Jesus, so that in the ages to come
He might show the surpassing riches of His grace
in kindness toward us in Christ Jesus.
For by grace you have been saved through faith;
and that not of yourselves, *it is* **the gift of God;**
(Ephesians 2:4-8 NASB1995)

Hannah was our fourth hire in April of 2021. Always with a smile and giggle, she brought immediate joy into Well Grounded. She was also an Exodus mom and was highly recommended by the other baristas. We interviewed two Exodus moms for one position, and Hannah basically told us we would hire her. And we did!

In the beginning, I watched her from a distance and was not sure of her. Hannah was a sidekick to the other baristas. I found it difficult to take her seriously. Was she committed to change? Was she ready for the required sacrifices to create a different future for herself and her boys? Just like the woman at the well, I was skeptical if she was "for real."

Three months in, I remained skeptical of Hannah's "grit" to make a lasting change for herself and her boys. At a customer appreciation event at the Coffee House, a reporter came and began interviewing the baristas. When it was Hannah's turn, the reporter asked her, "Hannah, what happened in your life; did you get in with the wrong crowd?" Hannah's immediate response was, "Oh, no, Ma'am! I WAS the wrong crowd!" That one comment convinced me that Hannah was ready to "own" her stuff. No victim mentality for this one.

After that, Hannah began sharing ideas to better Well Grounded, even creating new menu items. She became a person not swayed by others, not a sidekick, but a leader. And in January of 2022, her son, Evan, moved back in with her!

Hannah advanced higher and higher at Well Grounded, and at her third advancement, she was named Creative Director! Hannah now creates all our monthly specials. The level of leadership Hannah has attained thus far is tremendous. The other baristas look to her as an example of wisdom and success. She recently received her Manager's Certificate and moved to a salaried position at Well Grounded, which we call Barista Mentor. In addition to this, Hannah is now on the leadership team and is a part of every decision made to further the mission of giving second chances to marginalized women!

> "Then, leaving her water jar, the woman went back to the town and said to the people, 'Come, see a man who told me everything I ever did. Could this be the Messiah?' They came out of the town and made their way toward him."
> (John 4:28-30 NIV)

As the Woman at the Well went from shame to fame, Hannah has made decision after decision that has moved her from an old life of drugs and prison to a new life of leader and mentor.

Hannah's Advice:

If you are serious about changing your future, you have to change the people you hang out with, the environments you spend time in, and the activities/habits you engage in. Total change.

In Christ, Hannah is seen, safe, and significant.

**Mentoring other women —
This is Hannah's Victory Story!**

Tell a New Story. Tell a Better Story. Tell a Victory Story!

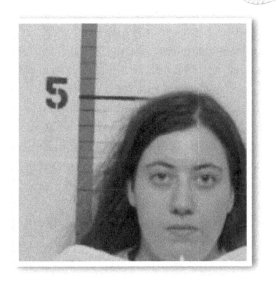

DAY 13

Baby Hanna's Story:
Feeling Insignificant

"Before I formed you in the womb I knew you,
before you were born I set you apart;
I appointed you as a prophet to the nations."
(Jeremiah 1:5 NIV)

Hanna was born in Quinlan, TX, the middle child with an older half-brother and a younger sister. During her childhood, she remembers her parents being together on and off, but they never married. Hanna also remembers moving around a lot and living with grandparents at times. In each home, she experienced a lot of instability, yelling, and anger. She never knew from moment to moment what kind of mood the "house" would be in. Heavy drinking was the norm, and the kids were included in the parties. Hanna started drinking around twelve years old.

Feeling anxious and vulnerable, Hanna would attempt to protect herself by hiding in her room. It was at this age she first began having feelings of depression. She felt so alone, with no one to help her. Hanna started partying with school friends at age sixteen, drinking and smoking pot every weekend. She looked forward to the weekends but, through the week, felt depressed and wanted to sleep all the time. Consequently, she was late to school every day and even skipped school a lot, although miraculously, she managed to make straight A's on her report cards.

Once Hanna graduated and moved out on her own, she got a job and started college. Unfortunately, her college experience only lasted three weeks. Her party life took over, and she spent all her money on pot and alcohol, after which she had to move into her grandma's house.

Questions: Have you experienced loneliness in your life?

Have you experienced depression?

When you feel lonely or depressed, do you hide or seek people to be around?

The lie: I am unlovable. Nobody sees me. I am utterly alone.

The truth:

> God is our refuge and strength,
>   an ever-present help in trouble.
> Therefore we will not fear, though the earth give way
>   and the mountains fall into the heart of the sea,
> though its waters roar and foam
>   and the mountains quake with their surging.
> There is a river whose streams make glad the city of God,
>   the holy place where the Most High dwells.
> God is within her, she will not fall;
>   God will help her at break of day. (Psalm 46:1-5 NIV)

Prayer: Father God, You are with me always. I am never alone. May Your Spirit, the Helper, fill me and comfort me. I surrender to Your care. You are sufficient. You are more than enough. Amen.

DAY 14

Baby Hanna's Story:
Attempting Sobriety

"Trust in the LORD with all your heart
And do not lean on your own understanding.
In all your ways acknowledge Him,
And He will make your paths straight."
(Proverbs 3:5-6 NASB1995)

With the failed attempt at college and the disappointment it brought, Hanna turned even more to alcohol, drinking every night either with friends or alone. She was working on and off, mostly with DoorDash, just to make enough money to purchase alcohol.

This dark season lasted for four years. Then came Hanna's first cry for help, and she was accepted to The Magdalen House, an addiction recovery program. She was able to complete the program but quickly relapsed. Hanna was in what felt like an endless cycle of addiction and depression. She would attend church on and off, have spurts of sobriety, then cycle back to drinking. The alcohol was the medicine she needed to push away the guilt and feelings of depression and aloneness.

One year later, she went back to The Magdalen House with better success and then graduated to a sober living community. While at the sober living home, she was hired by Well Grounded.

Questions: Have you tried to get help in a program or with counseling?

Do you consider this help successful?

It often takes several tries and a lot of follow-up support to successfully live life out of the darkness. Are you willing to keep trying?

The lie: I am helpless. I cannot do this. I will always fail.

The truth: "Blessed is the one who perseveres under trial because, having stood the test, that person will receive the crown of life that the Lord has promised to those who love him." (James 1:12 NIV)

Prayer: Father, in my own strength, I cannot do this. In Your strength, I can. No matter how many times I fall down, You are always here for me, like a kind Father. I will persevere. I will receive the crown of life. Amen.

DAY 15

Baby Hanna's Story:
Finding Freedom

But God,
being rich in mercy, because of His great love with
which He loved us, even when we were dead in our
transgressions, made us alive together with Christ
(by grace you have been saved), and raised us up with
Him, and seated us with Him in the heavenly *places*
in Christ Jesus, so that in the ages to come
He might show the surpassing riches of His grace in
kindness toward us in Christ Jesus.
For by grace you have been saved through faith;
and that not of yourselves, *it is* the gift of God;
(Ephesians 2:4-8 NASB1995)

Hanna was our first "walk-in" hire. Although she had gone through the recovery program at the Magdalen House and was living in a group home for recovering addicts, she came to us directly and asked for an interview. Hanna was sweet, fun, and immediately easy to love. She learned barista skills quickly. For the first two months, we were pinching ourselves. There were no visible signs of the woundedness that was always a part of hiring a new barista. Hanna's wounds were buried deeper.

Hanna worked hard and learned fast. She was a joy to be around and very encouraging to the other baristas. Then, one day, Hanna didn't show up to work at her scheduled time. We called and texted with no response for hours. Finally, she texted us that she felt paralyzed with fear and couldn't get out of bed that morning. This began happening more and more often. Finally, Hanna left completely and did not respond to any of us when we reached out. Months went by. We grieved her loss deeply. Several of us continued to send her love through texts, but she never responded.

Then, one wonderful day, three of us received a text from Hanna. We were so excited. We immediately scheduled to have lunch with her. From here we began rebuilding our relationships. Hanna was living in a trailer on her dad's property about forty-five minutes east of Dallas. As time went by, she restarted a 12-step program and sought help from a counselor.

Hanna's big breakthrough came when she got help for her depression. Although accepting the depression diagnosis was a humbling step for her, it also came with relief and hope. Since then, Hanna has experienced healing, freedom, and joy. She is now in full-time ministry. She is a light in the darkness.

We have continued to connect with Hanna and she has attended several of our Coffee House Events. She is an inspiration of perseverance through the dark days.

"May the God of hope fill you with all joy and peace as you trust in him, so that you may overflow with hope by the power of the Holy Spirit."
(Romans 15:13 NIV)

Hanna's Advice:

It may seem dark right now, and the only prayer you may be able to get out is "Jesus help me." Say it anyway. That is the beginning of surrender. Surrender is not always an all at once thing; it can be a process. You have a heavenly Father who loves you more than you can imagine, and there is so much He has in store for you. Seek Him. Seek His Word. Trust Him. Transformation is truly possible. There is a new life full of joy waiting on the other side of your mustard seed prayer. Begin to put your trust in Jesus and see what happens.

In Christ, Hanna is seen, safe, and significant.

Helping others accept and learn to live with a mental illness — This is Hanna's Victory Story!

Tell a New Story. Tell a Better Story. Tell a Victory Story!

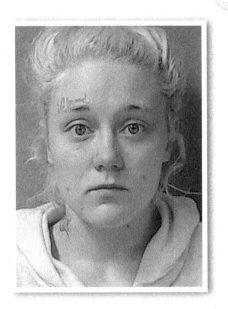

DAY 16

Taylor's Story:
No Boundaries/No Safety

The LORD is my rock, my fortress and my deliverer;
my God is my rock, in whom I take refuge,
my shield and the horn of my salvation.
He is my stronghold, my refuge and my savior—
from violent people you save me.
(2 Samuel 22:2-3 NIV)

Taylor was born in Powell, WY, but raised in a small West Texas town called Kermit. Her family was broken and divided from Taylor's earliest memory and continues to be broken today. She has two sisters — one adopted sister and an older biological sister. Her adopted sister became a medical doctor. Taylor has not been in contact with her for some time. Her biological sister has struggled with addiction her entire life. Taylor has no memories of her dad being around when she was very young. Her only memory was meeting him once when she was twelve years old. She never saw him again. Similar to Natasha's father, he was a ghost-like figure who appeared once and then disappeared from her life forever. What she knows about him is that he was in and out of prison and has continued on this path even today.

Taylor's mom was also in and out of prison, and Taylor lived with her aunt much of the time. One of her earliest memories was when she was five years old, and there was a knock at the door. When she opened the door, she found the Federal Marshals. Taylor watched as her mom was taken to prison.

Looking back, Taylor describes her life as "busy" as she was the caretaker of her four younger cousins. Taylor did not have the opportunity to "be a child." She assumed an adult role at a very young age, and it seemed to Taylor that every adult she knew did some kind of drugs. Along with the drugs, Taylor's aunt also physically and emotionally abused her.

Her granny "rescued" her when she was able to from the harsh punishments delivered by her aunt. Although Taylor's granny was also using drugs, she says her granny was her "safe person," a bit of light in her darkness. She was kind to Taylor.

Questions: Who in your life is a "safe person?"

What is it about that person that makes him/her safe to you?

Do you consider yourself to be a "safe person" to anyone, a light in their darkness?

The lie: I am helpless. Everyone uses drugs to get by. This is the only way I can make it.

The truth: "Do not get drunk on wine, which leads to debauchery. Instead, be filled with the Spirit." (Ephesians 5:18 NIV)

Prayer: Father God, YOU are my safe place. Please bring people into my life who love You and are seeking YOUR way of life. Let me be filled with You and not with alcohol, drugs, or any other temporary fix. You are my forever fix. Amen.

DAY 17

Taylor's Story: Prison

**"I will say of the LORD,
'He is my refuge and my fortress,
my God, in whom I trust.'"
(Psalm 91:2 NIV)**

The physical and emotional abuse continued through Taylor's childhood, and then Taylor experienced a series of other traumatizing events. The first was sexual abuse from one of her aunt's boyfriends and sexual harassment by several others.

The next trauma came in the form of loss to death. Forever seeking love, Taylor met a guy when she was sixteen. He was twenty-three years old and leading a life of drugs and crime. Taylor remembers that he was being pursued for a drug crime and was shot by the cops nine times in a chase.

Later, another friend, Joseph, whom Taylor had known since she was twelve years old, was pulled over by the police. Joseph made a rash decision to swallow all the drugs he had on him so the police wouldn't arrest him, but when he was released and went to the apartment where Taylor was staying, he died from an overdose in her arms.

With so much abuse and trauma, Taylor felt lonely, misunderstood, and lost. She believed she was destined to fail and that she was broken, dirty, and unlovable. It was at this low point that she became involved with smuggling illegal aliens to make money. When she was caught, she spent two years in a federal prison called Carswell in Fort Worth, TX.

For many, prison is a terrifying experience. For Taylor, prison felt "freeing." The time there helped her get clean and find God. During her time in prison, she was able to build a solid, distraction-free relationship with Him. In prison, Taylor surrendered to the Lord and got honest with herself. However, when she got out, her newfound freedom didn't last long. In Taylor's words, "I didn't change my people, places, or things!" She quickly relapsed into the familiar world of drugs and crime and became pregnant. She was arrested and court-ordered to rehab. This court order took Taylor to Dallas, TX, and later into a program called In My Shoes.

Questions: Has trauma been a part of your story?

Have you been able to process this trauma with a safe person/counselor?

The lie: I am broken and unlovable.

The truth: "The sacrifices of God are a broken spirit; a broken and contrite heart, O God, you will not despise." (Psalm 51:17 NASB1995)

Prayer: Lord, I am broken but not unlovable. It is in humility that You draw near, so let my brokenness be my strength. When I am weak, YOU are strong. I rest in You. Amen.

DAY 18
Taylor's Story:
Safety in Christ

But God,
being rich in mercy, because of His great love with
which He loved us, even when we were dead in our
transgressions, made us alive together with Christ
(by grace you have been saved), and raised us up with
Him, and seated us with Him in the heavenly *places*
in Christ Jesus, so that in the ages to come
He might show the surpassing riches of His grace
in kindness toward us in Christ Jesus.
For by grace you have been saved through faith;
and that not of yourselves, *it is* the gift of God;
(Ephesians 2:4-8 NASB1995)

In the Spring of 2022, Well Grounded hired Taylor from one of our hiring partners called In My Shoes, a Catholic organization in Oak Cliff, TX, that takes in pregnant homeless women. Taylor was seven months pregnant when we met her. She was hardworking and a very fast learner. Smart and wise beyond her twenty-three years, Taylor told us in her interview that she had learned that "your secrets will keep you sick." She had made a decision to build an honest and open life. We were able to be a close part of Taylor's pregnancy, birth, and delivery, and Taylor returned to work at Well Grounded once baby Nova was accepted into a daycare center.

Taylor's postpartum proved more challenging than any of us could have imagined, and she struggled with her emotions and decisions. Thankfully, she was accepted into Exodus Ministries, where she found a home and much support. However, her postpartum depression threatened to take her back to those dark places. Her poor decision making led her to rashly quit work at Well Grounded and become pregnant again. It seemed that Taylor would spin back down her previous path.

With so much grace from Exodus and the Well Grounded Coffee Family, we held her steady and helped her get back on the path of light and victory. Taylor was rehired at Well Grounded and gave birth to a baby boy in the Summer of 2023.

Taylor is now nearly two years sober and no longer caged to her past. She completed a Christ-centered twelve step program called Re:generation and then moved into leadership within the program. She has two healthy children. She celebrated one year at Well Grounded in the Spring of 2023. She is learning and growing and puts God first.

Taylor says what has helped her most is being honest with herself, having a good support group, and, most of all, God. She says she is not so negative now. Instead, she turns to God and positive, supportive people. She tries to bear all the fruit of the spirit!

With the supportive people and programs around her, Taylor has bought a car, started college, and graduated from Exodus ministries! Taylor was accepted into Restored Hope's apartments, where she can continue in a supportive community and focus on her college classes. She hopes to earn a master's degree in Drug Abuse Counseling and eventually help teens who have lived the life she used to live.

Taylor's Advice:

We must withstand the rain if we wish to see the sun.

In Christ, Taylor is seen, safe, and significant.

Creating and teaching safe boundaries — This is Taylor's Victory Story!

Tell a New Story. Tell a Better Story. Tell a Victory Story!

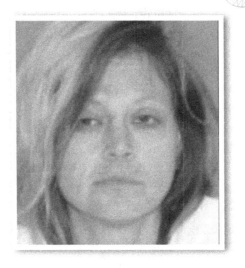

DAY 19

Amber's Story:
Drowning in Shame

"So, my dear brothers and sisters,
be strong and immovable. Always work enthusiastically
for the Lord, for you know that nothing you do for the
Lord is ever useless."
(1 Corinthians 15:58 NLT)

NATALIE HUSCHECK & THE WELL GROUNDED SISTERHOOD

Amber was born in Bellflower, CA, the first daughter of her mom. Her parents never married, and they only stayed together until Amber was three months old. Her dad suffered addictions to both gambling and heroin. Her mom left him and flew with Amber to Texas when Amber was still a baby. Amber remembers growing up making yearly visits with her dad in a California prison for over twenty years. He would send letters and make promises but never fulfill them. Tragically, Amber's father died in prison on April 18th, 2022.

When Amber was three, her mom had a baby girl with an abusive boyfriend. Amber remembers him as a bit of a "Dr. Jekyll/Mr. Hyde." He would pop in and out bringing gifts but was also on drugs and was physically abusive.

Although Amber was raised by both her mom and grandma, her mom's addiction to drugs shadowed their lives. Her mom was eventually caught and spent time in prison for selling drugs. Amber stayed with her grandma. When Amber was thirteen, her grandma developed lung cancer. Amber felt like she was losing the only stable person in her life. She and her mom both became depressed. Whatever efforts her mom had been making to hide her drug life previously, ended with the death of her grandma. Amber's mom was suddenly open about her whole drug scene which included drugs, violence, and "old, perverted men" around Amber daily. Meth was cooked in the home. At age fourteen, Amber remembers being sexually groped by the many visitors.

Amber's relationship with her mom became increasingly abusive. Her mom would say cruel things such as "I hate you" and "You're worthless." Amber began "cutting" when she was fourteen. Her mom would punch and kick her and tell her she was stupid. At times, she would lock Amber out of the house. The abuse from her mom lasted from about age eight through age fifteen, when Amber moved in with a boyfriend and became pregnant. Her mom begged her to get an abortion, but Amber would not. Her mom would come by to physically abuse her to try to make her lose the baby. Despite the abuse, baby Tiffany was born in 2000.

Amber's boyfriend tried to provide and care for them. In the beginning, he was not abusive. However, when he lost his job, he began selling drugs to help them get by. Shortly after, they both began using. Then the physical abuse began. At age sixteen, Amber overdosed and nearly died. She remembers feeling outside of her body. The physical abuse escalated, and at times, her boyfriend would even hold a gun to Amber's head. Then they would get clean for a short period, and he would get a job.

The year 2004 brought another baby girl, Tara, and the couple decided to get married. Things were looking up until they began drinking again. With the alcohol, the physical abuse returned. Amber remembers calling her mom for help, but her mom told her she "deserved it." Amber felt she had no one to help her. When her husband went to jail for an episode of extreme abuse, they separated; Amber and the two girls went to stay with her mom. She continued using meth on and off.

Questions: Who in your life has made promises but never fulfilled them?

Has anyone broken your trust?

How did that make you feel?

How difficult is it for you to trust people?

The lie: I am helpless. There is no hope, only darkness.

The truth: "May the God of hope fill you with all joy and peace in believing, so that by the power of the Holy Spirit you may abound in hope." (Romans 15:13 ESV)

Prayer: Father God, You are all light, all peace, and all joy. When I am in darkness, lift my eyes to You, speak Your Truth into my life, and give me hope. YOU are my hope. Amen.

DAY 20

Amber's Story:
Spiraling Down

"Dear friends, now we are children of God,
and what we will be has not yet been made known.
But we know that when Christ appears,
we shall be like him, for we shall see him as he is.
Our identity as a child of God means that we rely
fully on God and trust in His plan for our lives."
(1 John 3:2 NIV)

With her husband in jail, Amber met another guy and soon gave birth to a son named Trey. They lived together for three years, during which time she continued to do drugs. Although the boyfriend did not do drugs with Amber, he drank alcohol heavily.

Then Amber was arrested for possession of drugs and spent five months in jail. When she was released on a PR bond (personal recognizance), she headed straight to the streets. She was picked up again, facing 2-20 years, and this time she begged for help. Amber was granted rehab but couldn't seem to make it work. She was kicked out of two different rehabilitation programs.

After several months of using and living with another abusive guy who almost strangled her to death, she says she "woke up" and knew she needed God's help. Amber called a friend who connected her to a ministry called Restored Hope. Other programs hadn't helped. For Amber, they were too short and lacked a faith-based foundation. Restored Hope is a three year program. It was during her second year in the program that Well Grounded hired her. She graduated part two of Restored Hope in December 2022.

Question: Have you spent much of your life single (without a romantic partner), or do you feel you always need someone and cannot make it on your own?

Do you look to a romantic partner for security? Self-worth? Identity?

The lie: I am worthless. The street and drugs are the only life I know. I am stuck here.

The truth: "Therefore, if anyone is in Christ, he is a new creation. The old has passed away; behold, the new has come." (2 Corinthians 5:17 ESV)

Prayer: Father, let the old pass away and create a new life in me. Heal me, teach me, and guide me into safe places. Be my shelter and bring me to new friends who are living a new life. Amen.

DAY 21

Amber's Story:
Finding Freedom & Self-Love

But God,
being rich in mercy, because of His great love with
which He loved us, even when we were dead in our
transgressions, made us alive together with Christ
(by grace you have been saved), and raised us up with
Him, and seated us with Him in the heavenly *places*
in Christ Jesus, so that in the ages to come
He might show the surpassing riches of
His grace in kindness toward us in Christ Jesus.
For by grace you have been saved through faith;
and that not of yourselves, *it is* **the gift of God;**
(Ephesians 2:4-8 NASB1995)

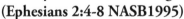

Amber was our first hire from an organization that rescues women from domestic violence and sex trafficking. She was barely alive when she showed up at their doorsteps. In some ways, she was as strong as nails and possibly the hardest worker we ever hired. In other ways, she was excruciatingly fragile.

Amber was committed to change. She fit in well with the team and advanced to Tier II Barista, taking on new responsibilities. Amber loved BIG and hugged everyone!

We helped Amber move into a sober living house with other recovering addicts. She was rebuilding family relationships when a situation occurred in Amber's life which caused her to stumble. What would seem to be a blessing, a large settlement from the death of her father, caused Amber to spiral into darkness. She spent the entire settlement within a two-month period, spending which took her back into danger and drugs. We pleaded with Amber to get help, but it wasn't until she had a scare with Fentanyl that she reached out and allowed us to help her get back into rehab.

After 28 days in rehab, Amber moved in with her mom so she could re-establish relationships with her three children. She is working hard to heal family relationships and on her sobriety. Amber comes by regularly to the coffee house to stay in touch and to share her BIG love and hugs with the team.

Amber's Advice:

You are worthy of love. You are worth fighting for. "You can do all things through Christ who strengthens you." (Philippians 4:13 NKJV) Don't ever give in, and never ever give up on yourself. Learn to love yourself. If I can do it, you can too!

In Christ, Amber is seen, safe, and significant.

Building a strong foundation— This is Amber's Victory Story!

Tell a New Story. Tell a Better Story. Tell a Victory Story!

DAY 22

Jessica's Story:
Used and Abused

**"When we were utterly helpless, Christ came at just the
right time and died for us sinners."
(Romans 5:6 NLT)**

Jessica was born in Shreveport, LA, the second daughter of her parents. She recalls that when her parents were together, life seemed good. Unfortunately, her dad went to prison when she was only five years old for a drug charge. This was when her life took a terrible turn. She suddenly became a pawn in her mom's addiction, and her mom began selling her to men to get drug money.

This continued for several years. Jessica's dad's family tried to step in, but her mom wouldn't allow it. Eventually, her mom completely abandoned her. Her sister was eight years older than Jessica and had already left home.

Jessica went to the police about the abuse and her current situation. They placed her in the care of her aunt and uncle on her dad's side. Sadly, this situation was even worse for Jessica. The abuse was extreme. Since drugs had been introduced to her at age eight, she continued to use them to numb herself.

Life was very difficult with continual trauma. Then she was sent to a boarding academy for a year, a time Jessica remembers as the best and safest of her life. This year was like a welcome respite for her, and she dreaded having to return home when the year ended.

Jessica's mom OD'd alone in an RV trailer when Jess was only sixteen. She had been dead for days when Jessica found her.

Question: Has someone died who you were very close to?

How did you handle the death?

Are you still grieving?

The lie: I am worthless, not worthy of being loved and cared for.

The truth: "I have loved you with an everlasting love; I have drawn you with unfailing kindness." (Jeremiah 31:3 NIV)

Prayer: God, You are my good, good Father. Your Word says You love me. I don't understand it, but I receive it. All of it. Pour out Your lavish love on me and heal me. Help me know that I am worthy because You have declared me worthy through my Savior, Jesus. Amen.

DAY 23

Jessica's Story: Head Under Water

**"May your unfailing love be my comfort,
according to your promise to your servant."
(Psalm 119: 76 NIV)**

Jessica's life continued to be marked with abuse and abandonment. She met a guy at a bike rally and became pregnant at age eighteen. Her life was so unstable that the child was taken from her, and the relationship did not last. Jessica describes her life as feeling stuck, like her head was under water.

She then met a guy who owned a strip club and had two baby girls with him. Soon after, he was shot and killed. Jess ran off, leaving her daughters behind. She was mentally unstable and began selling her body. She became pregnant again and, this time, gave the baby up for adoption. She continued life on the streets, still feeling like her head was under water.

With another relationship came another baby, Enoch. This time, Jessica was determined to keep him. The father went to jail, and with no support, she ran off with a drug handler and became pregnant with another boy. Jessica was on the verge of losing the two boys due to an extensive stint of drug use when she chose to enter a 122-day rehab. The boys went into foster care.

The rehab was refreshing for Jessica because she knew she didn't have to wake up and live that kind of life again. It was there she decided to change her people, places, and things and start all over with only the clothes on her back.

Question: Have you ever made the decision to start over?

What would it look like to begin brand new and make better choices?

The lie: I am helpless. My life will always be darkness, abuse, and abandonment.

The truth: "This I recall to my mind, Therefore I have hope. The Lord's loving kindnesses indeed never cease, For His compassions never fail. They are new every morning; Great is Your faithfulness. 'The Lord is my portion,' says my soul, 'Therefore I have hope in Him.'" (Lamentations)

Prayer: Father God, You are my hope. You are my light in darkness. May I cling to You when I am afraid, when I doubt, when I feel alone. Your loving kindness will never end. Let me meditate on that now and always. Amen.

DAY 24

Jessica's Story: Finding Stability

But God,
being rich in mercy, because of His great love with
which He loved us, even when we were dead in our
transgressions, made us alive together with Christ
(by grace you have been saved), and raised us up
with Him, and seated us with Him in the heavenly
places **in Christ Jesus, so that in the ages to come He**
might show the surpassing riches of His grace
in kindness toward us in Christ Jesus.
For by grace you have been saved through faith;
and that not of yourselves, *it is* **the gift of God;**
(Ephesians 2:4-8 NASB1995)

Jessica completed rehab and earned back full custody of her two boys. They were staying at a sober living home for moms when we interviewed and hired her at Well Grounded. She started work in the Spring of 2022.

Jessica was adjusting well, learning skills and work ethic when she hit a snag. She found out she was pregnant again. This would be three babies under the age of three. We encouraged her to consider adoption for the new baby so that she could focus on the other two boys, but Jessica felt she had lost enough children and was set on raising all three.

Knowing she would need a higher level of support and accountability, we challenged her to apply to Exodus Ministries. Miraculously, she was accepted into the program even though they had never accepted anyone who was pregnant before. She received an incredible amount of support from the staff and other moms throughout her pregnancy and after.

Jessica continued working at Well Grounded, and although the progress was slow, she achieved several milestones, including completing one year of working with us, promotion to Tier II barista, two years clean, and graduation from Exodus. In addition to all of this, she began college classes and was accepted into a supportive program for single moms seeking an education. Jessica continues to stay connected with the Well Grounded family, and her three boys are growing and thriving.

Jessica's Advice:

In order to prosper, you have to let go and keep your eyes forward because your past can keep you from your brightest future!

In Christ, Jessica is seen, safe, and significant.

**Trusting the support of a "Sisterhood" —
This is Jessica's Victory Story!**

Tell a New Story. Tell a Better Story. Tell a Victory Story!

DAY 25

Olympia's Story: Drugs & Abuse

"But he said to me, 'My grace is sufficient for you, for my power is made perfect in weakness.' Therefore I will boast all the more gladly about my weaknesses, so that Christ's power may rest on me." (2 Corinthians 12:9 NIV)

Olympia was born in Monroe, LA, the second child of twelve and the oldest of seven girls. She felt blessed to have both parents in her life growing up and remembers all the fun of growing up with so many siblings. Olympia describes her childhood as "simply wonderful." She greatly admired her father, who passed away in 2010.

She met a young man who initially treated her with kindness and respect. However, after they were together for several years and had four children together, drugs began to change his behavior, and he became abusive. Olympia also started using drugs to cope with the sexual abuse from her children's father. Her life suddenly went downhill. The constant abuse made her feel broken in every aspect of her life. She felt broken spiritually, physically, mentally, and emotionally; she felt there was no way out. During their time together, Olympia gave birth to ten children, six boys and four girls.

The sexual abuse of her children's father and his friends took her under and to a very dark place in her life. In Olympia's words, "physically, I was present, but mentally, I was gone."

Questions: Was your childhood mostly happy, mostly sad, or a mixture of both?

What is one happy childhood memory that makes you smile?

The lie: I am helpless. There is no way out. I'm stuck.

The truth: "For freedom Christ has set us free; stand firm therefore, and do not submit again to a yoke of slavery." (Galatians 5:1 ESV)

Prayer: Lord, when I feel stuck, remind me You have a way out. Reveal to me Your plan of freedom, and let me place my trust and my hope in You. You are freedom. You are light and life. Fill me with hope. Amen.

DAY 26

Olympia's Story: Recovery

"So if the Son sets you free, you will be free indeed."
(John 8:36 ESV)

Olympia went into recovery many times over a period of eighteen years but always relapsed. She continued using drugs to cope with the abuse, but in the end, the drugs didn't help. She finally realized she needed God more than drugs.

She came to Texas in August of 2021 to a friend's home to escape the abuse. It was there that she went to a program called Nexus for 90 days of detox and recovery. After Nexus, she was accepted into Exodus Ministries, hired by Well Grounded, and was trying to regain custody of her youngest daughter. Sadly, Olympia relapsed within three weeks of leaving the program.

As she was walking to the grocery store one day, a man walked by her, opened his hand and showed her some pills. That was all it took. In an instant, she was high and back on the streets, chasing her next fix. Full surrender and the belief that there could be a better life were still too difficult to grasp. She disappeared from Exodus and from Well Grounded and was gone for five days. We had no idea where she was and feared the very worst.

Question: What gives you hope?

Do you believe in a better future?

What would that better future look like?

The lie: I am unlovable. Only drugs can give me relief from my problems and help with the emotional pain.

The truth: "No temptation has overtaken you except what is common to mankind. And God is faithful; he will not let you be tempted beyond what you can bear. But when you are tempted, he will also provide a way out so that you can endure it." (1 Corinthians 10:13 NIV)

Prayer: Father, I confess that so often I forget to call on You when I'm in need. I spend so much time in worry and struggle until I finally remember You are there. Father, I cry out to You right now. Save me from the brokenness of the world and the brokenness of myself. In You, I am whole. Amen.

DAY 27

Olympia's Story: Finding Her "Glow"

But God,
being rich in mercy, because of His great love with
which He loved us, even when we were dead in our
transgressions, made us alive together with Christ
(by grace you have been saved), and raised us up with
Him, and seated us with Him in the heavenly
places in Christ Jesus, so that in the ages to come
He might show the surpassing riches of
His grace in kindness toward us in Christ Jesus.
For by grace you have been saved through faith;
and that not of yourselves, *it is* the gift of God;
(Ephesians 2:4-8 NASB1995)

After five days, Olympia somehow found the courage to walk through the doors of Well Grounded. The relief we felt was overwhelming as we surrounded her with love, grace, and hugs. Exodus accepted her back, and she returned to Nexus for another 90 days of rehab.

This time, she began to do things differently. She really worked the program the second time through and was released July 2nd, 2022. Olympia has been clean ever since. She has continued to make changes and depend on God more than her own understanding. She asked God to be her guide and felt He did just that.

Olympia says what has helped most is "putting God first and having a loving and caring support system." She is very careful about the people she lets into her circle.

At Well Grounded, Olympia has been promoted to Tier II Barista and celebrated a year of work. She regained custody of her youngest daughter and is re-establishing her relationships with her older children. She graduated from Exodus and moved into her own apartment. She is now a peer advocate, speaking to other women about what she went through and how she came out of it. Olympia is clean and sober today!

Her plan is to work and regain a driver's license so she can buy a car. Her greatest hope is to have all her kids back with her and to spend Thanksgiving and Christmas together.

She says she feels great to be herself again. She is learning to love herself and to feel beautiful again. She challenges herself to find her identity in Christ and to allow herself to start growing and changing things in her life.

Olympia's Advice:

Find your strength in God and find a loving support group to walk with you on your journey.

In Christ, Olympia is seen, safe, and significant.

**Trusting God for her children —
This is Olympia's Victory Story!**

Tell a New Story. Tell a Better Story. Tell a Victory Story!

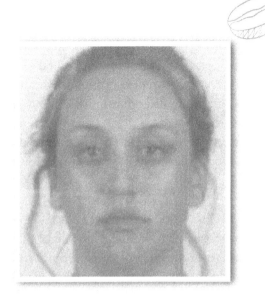

DAY 28
Jessica's Story:
Taking Care of Everyone Else

"For I know the plans I have for you,"
declares the LORD, "plans to prosper you and not to
harm you, plans to give you hope and a future."
(Jeremiah 29:11 NIV)

Jessica was born in Mission Hills, CA, to a single, nineteen year old mom. Jessica's dad was in the military and not ready to settle down, so her parents never married. She was mostly raised by her grandma and grew up spending more time with her grandma than her mom. Jessica's mom was often out partying and rarely around. Jessica felt abandoned by her, and most of the words she received from her mom were harsh and emotionally abusive.

At age five, Jessica's world turned darker when an older neighbor sexually abused her. Not long after that, she was sexually abused again, this time by her stepdad. Jessica remembers her stepdad as controlling and vindictive. He would randomly do mean things, such as break her music CDs. Together, her mom and stepdad had three more children. They divorced when Jessica was fourteen years old. Jessica, her mom, and three siblings moved back in with her grandma. She remembers feeling scared and anxious most of the time. Her grandma was her one safe person.

For the next two years, her mom's partying increased dramatically. Jessica moved into the parenting role and cared for her siblings. Her grandma had a debilitating stroke, and Jessica became her caretaker as well. This was when she started taking some of her grandma's pain pills to cope with the pressures in her life. This opened the doorway to more drug experimentation.

Meanwhile, Jessica's Mom found an online boyfriend and moved away, taking only the two youngest kids. Her brother went to live with his dad, leaving Jessica abandoned once again with her sick grandma. She dropped out of high school to care for her grandma and enrolled in independent study.

Questions: In what ways were you forced to grow up too fast?

In what ways do you sometimes still act like a child?

The lie: I am worthless. It is my responsibility to take care of everyone around me, even my own neglect.

The truth: "Come to Me, all who are weary and heavy-laden, and I will give you rest. Take My yoke upon you and learn from Me, for I am gentle and humble in heart, and you will find rest for your souls. For My yoke is easy and My burden is light." (Matthew 11:28-30 NASB1995)

Prayer: God, show me the way of rest. Teach me to "take up Your yoke" and find soul rest. I am weary of striving and never gaining ground. I need a different way, Your way. I surrender to You. Amen.

DAY 29

Jessica's Story: Jail and Addiction

What, then, shall we say in response to these things? If God is for us, who can be against us? He who did not spare his own Son, but gave him up for us all—how will he not also, along with him, graciously give us all things? Who will bring any charge against those whom God has chosen? It is God who justifies. Who then is the one who condemns? No one. Christ Jesus who died—more than that, who was raised to life—is at the right hand of God and is also interceding for us. Who shall separate us from the love of Christ? Shall trouble or hardship or persecution or famine or nakedness or danger or sword? As it is written:

"For your sake we face death all day long;
we are considered as sheep to be slaughtered."

No, in all these things we are more than conquerors
through him who loved us. For I am convinced
that neither death nor life, neither angels nor
demons,[b] neither the present nor the future, nor
any powers, neither height nor depth, nor anything
else in all creation, will be able to separate us from
the love of God that is in Christ Jesus our Lord.

(Romans 8:31-38 NIV)

Jessica's grandma's health declined, and she moved into a nursing facility. Jessica stayed at her grandma's house with a boyfriend. They started partying more and moved other questionable people into the house. The situation spiraled downward, and the house ended up in foreclosure.

As her life spun further and further out of control, Jessica was caught and charged with stealing and heroin possession in the state of California. She spent three months in jail. When she got out, she went right back into the drug scene. Jessica called her mom for help, and her mom came and helped her get clean. After that, she did use alcohol to help numb her emotional pain on a daily basis, but she stopped doing drugs.

Jessica started working at a bowling alley and dating a coworker. Early in the relationship, she became pregnant and gave birth to her daughter, Rayne, in June of 2015. Unfortunately, there was a lot of tension between this boyfriend and his family. When the tension became too much, Jessica again called her mom for rescue. Although her mom was now living in Texas with a new husband she had met online, she did come to get Jessica and the baby.

Jessica began to spiral into a deep depression. She had frequent fights with her mom and was drinking a lot. She then began to take pills she would find around the house. Jessica would try to earn her mom's love by working hard around the house, but it never seemed enough, and she was met with the familiar emotional abuse.

Then Jessica met another guy. She would sneak out at night and steal her mom's car to be with him. Soon they started using meth together. This relationship lasted five years and ended with a second pregnancy, a little boy.

Her poor choices led to more time spent in county jail, this time in the state of Texas. Jessica remembers feeling angry and just wanting to be left alone. She worried about her kids a lot. When she got out, she tried to stay clean, but with little support, she quickly relapsed. Child Protection Services swooped in and removed Jessica from the house. Thankfully, they didn't take the kids. They were able to stay with her mom, but Jessica wasn't allowed at the house.

Jessica lived in her car for about 1½ years, and her life on the streets led to a third pregnancy. This time, she went to rehab, and after completion, gave birth to another son, Llyam.

Alone and chronically depressed, Jessica relapsed. Determined to turn her life around, she returned to rehab for 90 more days and then was accepted into transitional living with two of her children at Exodus Ministries.

Questions: Each of the women in this book had a turning point. Have you had a turning point?

If so, what did it look like?

The lie: I'm unlovable. No one will ever love, accept, and care for me.

The truth: "Do not be anxious about anything, but in every situation, by prayer and petition, with thanksgiving, present your requests to God." (Philippians 4:6 NIV)

Prayer: God, You are my Father. You will always love, accept, and care for me with a perfect love. You are enough. Comfort and heal me. Guide my every step. I receive ALL of Your love because You have decided I am worthy and lovable. Amen.

DAY 30

Jessica's Story: Finding Peace

But God,
being rich in mercy, because of His great love with
which He loved us, even when we were dead in our
transgressions, made us alive together with Christ
(by grace you have been saved), and raised us up with
Him, and seated us with Him in the heavenly
places in Christ Jesus, so that in the ages to come
He might show the surpassing riches of
His grace in kindness toward us in Christ Jesus.
For by grace you have been saved through faith;
and that not of yourselves, *it is* the gift of God;
(Ephesians 2:4-8 NASB1995)

Once at Exodus Ministries, Jessica reached out to Well Grounded for a job. She was highly recommended by the other baristas and proved to be a very hard worker. Initially, she was only hired to work occasional Saturdays; however, she was such a strong team member her hours were quickly increased.

As her life started to stabilize, Jessica made a commitment of faith and was baptized on April 24, 2022. She began living her life very differently. She says, "I try to have a Christ-like mindset — kind, giving, and forgiving." She attributes the biggest difference in her life to Jesus and her supportive network.

Jessica has been clean since January of 2022, has been promoted to Tier III Barista at the coffee house, and continues to grow and contribute greatly to the team.

She is so grateful to have two of her three children back and is working to build a relationship with her son, Jayce. She has enrolled in college classes and has proven to be an excellent student. Jessica plans to continue sharing the hope of Jesus with those in darkness.

Jessica's advice:

"God is big enough."

In Christ, Jessica is seen, safe, and significant.

**Learning that God is ENOUGH —
This is Jessica's Victory Story!**

Tell a New Story. Tell a Better Story. Tell a Victory Story!

DAY 31
Learning to HOPE

"Let us hold unswervingly to the hope we profess,
for he who promised is faithful."
(Hebrews 10:23 NIV)

Until the day we die, no one's story is fully written. And in the world of incredible woundedness and trauma, it often takes many trips around the sun to find the path of healing. Some baristas were not quite ready to enter the path of healing. Some of us think ourselves unworthy of love and healing.

Many of the previous stories have shown a life transformed by love, community, and healing. But we want to acknowledge that not all of our baristas have stayed on this path. Some have left and returned to drugs. Some have returned to prison. We continue to pray, reach out, and hope as God writes our stories.

Hope for tomorrow is power for today.

In Christ, YOU are seen, safe, and significant.

What will be YOUR Victory Story?

Tell a New Story. Tell a Better Story. Tell a Victory Story!

But God,
being rich in mercy, because of His great love with
which He loved us, even when we were dead in our
transgressions, made us alive together with Christ
(by grace you have been saved), and raised us up with
Him, and seated us with Him in the heavenly
places **in Christ Jesus, so that in the ages to come**
He might show the surpassing riches of
His grace in kindness toward us in Christ Jesus.
For by grace you have been saved through faith;
and that not of yourselves, *it is* **the gift of God;**
(Ephesians 2:4-8 NASB1995)

Our prayer is that your story has a "but God" in it.

www.wellgrounded.coffee

wellgroundedcoffeecommunity@gmail.com

FB: Well Grounded Coffee Co

IG: @wellgroundedcoffeeco

9219 Garland Rd #2109, Dallas, TX 75218

By purchasing more books or becoming a monthly donor, you can help us bring light to those in darkness, including individuals in prison, battling addiction, or experiencing abuse.

For every book you purchase, you're directly contributing to providing books to individuals in challenging situations.

Your support matters. You can be the change in someone's life today.

To learn more or take action, scan the QR code below.

Thank you for being a part of our mission to share hope and knowledge.

Printed in the USA
CPSIA information can be obtained
at www.ICGtesting.com
JSHW081119160224
57429JS00005B/16